How to make a Present

Paul Humphrey

Photography by Chris Fairclough

SEA-TO-SEA

Mankato Collingwood London

This edition first published in 2008 by
Sea-to-Sea Publications
1980 Lookout Drive
North Mankato
Minnesota 56003

Printed in China

Library of Congress Cataloging in Publication Data

Humphrey, Paul.
　How to make a present / by Paul Humphrey.
　　　p.cm. (Crafty kids)
　Includes index.
　ISBN 978-1-59771-103-6
　1. Bread dough craft--Juvenile literature. 2. Handicraft--Juvenile literature. I. Title.

TT880.H85 2007
745.5--dc22

2006050019

9 8 7 6 5 4 3 2

Published by arrangement with the Watts Publishing Group Ltd, London

Planning and production by Discovery Books Limited
Editor: Rachel Tisdale
Designer: Ian Winton
Photography: Chris Fairclough
Series advisors: Diana Bentley MA and Dee Reid MA,
Fellows of Oxford Brookes University

The author, packager, and publisher would like to thank Ottilie Austin-Baker for
her participation in this book.

Contents

What you need

Do you like dinosaurs?
Here's how to make a
dinosaur present!

These are the
things you
will need:

A large
mixing bowl

½ cup of salt

A pencil

2½ cups flour

A wooden
spoon

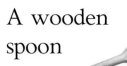

A table
knife

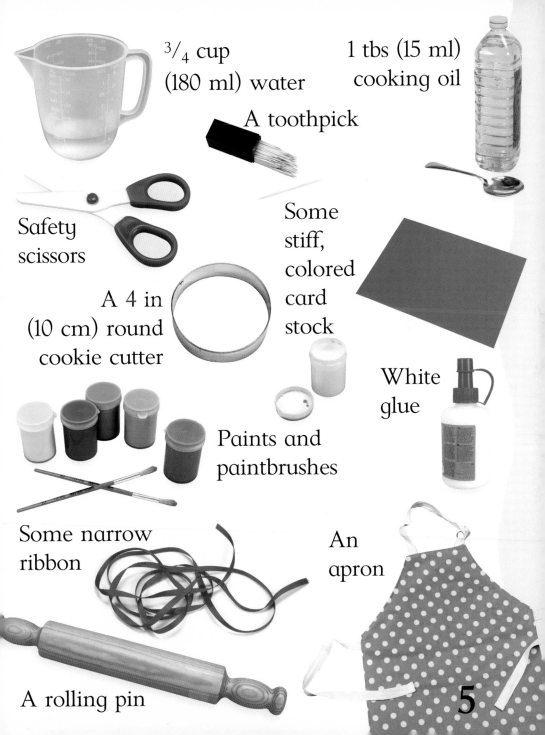

³/₄ cup (180 ml) water

1 tbs (15 ml) cooking oil

A toothpick

Safety scissors

Some stiff, colored card stock

A 4 in (10 cm) round cookie cutter

White glue

Paints and paintbrushes

Some narrow ribbon

An apron

A rolling pin

5

Drawing the dinosaur

First, draw a dinosaur shape like this onto the card stock.

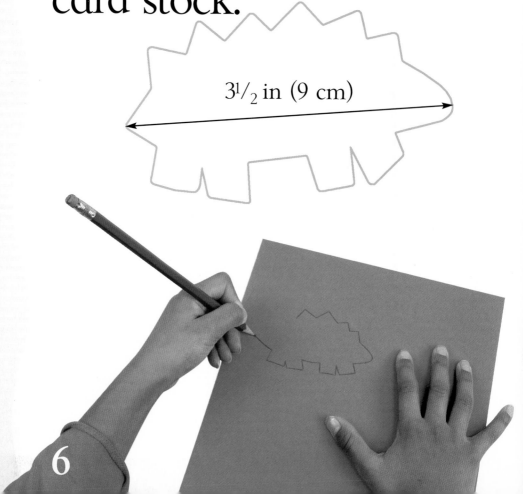

$3^{1}/_{2}$ in (9 cm)

Make it $3^1/_2$ in (9 cm) from head to tail.

Carefully cut out the dinosaur shape.

Making the dough

Next, put the flour and salt into the mixing bowl, and stir.

Pour in the water a little at a time.

Add the oil.

Keep stirring the sticky mixture.

Kneading the dough

Knead the mixture to make a smooth dough.

Spread some flour over the worktop.

Then roll out the dough until it is ¹/₄ in (6 mm) thick.

Cutting the dough

Cut out a circle of dough.

Press the cut-out dinosaur onto the leftover dough and cut around it.

13

Sticking the shapes together

Sprinkle some water over the dough circle.

Gently press the dough

dinosaur onto the circle.

15

Baking your present

Use the toothpick to make a hole at the top of the circle.

Make a face for your dinosaur.

Leave your present to dry for 2 to 3 days.

Or ask an adult to bake it at 250°F (130°C) for 8 hours.

Painting your present

When it is dry, paint your present with white paint. Leave it to dry.

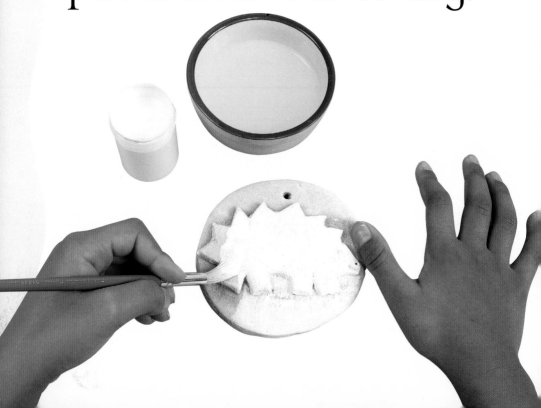

Next, paint the background and the dinosaur in bright colors.

Finishing your present

When the paint is dry, brush on two coats of white glue.

This stops the paint from coming off of your present.

Leave it to dry.

Wrapping your present

Thread the ribbon through the hole.

Finally, tie a knot to make a loop.

Now you can wrap
your dinosaur present
and give
it to a
friend.

Steps

Can you remember all of the steps to make your present?

1. Draw and cut out the shape.

2. Make the dough.

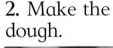

3. Cut the dough.

4. Press the pieces.

5. Make the face.

6. Bake the dough.

7. Paint the present.

8. Tie the ribbon.

9. Wrap the present.